CLASSICS

FOR THE YOUNG CLARINET PLAYER

CURNOW® MUSIC

Exclusively Distributed By

HAL•LEONARD® CORPORATION

7777 W. BLUEMOUND RD. P.O. BOX 13819 MILWAUKEE, WI 53213

T0050750

Order Number: CMP 0544-01-400

CLASSICS FOR THE YOUNG CLARINET PLAYER
Clarinet

ISBN 978-90-431-1407-3

CD number: 19-016-3 CMP

CLASSICS

FOR THE YOUNG CLARINET PLAYER

The music of the great masters has long been the object of study by musicians around the world. Unfortunately, many times the difficulty level makes this music inaccessible to the young musician. With our new publication, CLASSICS FOR THE YOUNG CLARINET PLAYER, music by Beethoven, Brahms, Clarke, Grieg, Haydn, Strauss, Mozart and Purcell has been arranged in a format that is appropriate for the young instrumentalist.

By simply dropping the accompanying CD into your CD player and selecting the proper CD track to match the music on the page of the book that you want to play, you are immediately able to not only play the music, but also play it with a real concert band accompaniment. This format provides an excellent opportunity to play the music with an accompaniment that is close in style and sound to the original. Playing this kind of music is an important part of the complete music education of all students, and will result in a well-rounded appreciation for music of many different styles. I am sure you will enjoy this new opportunity for music-making!

James Curnow

P.S.: These solos can also be performed with a live band playing. Each of them are available as concert band arrangements through Curnow Music Press.

PROGRAM NOTES

ALLEGRETTO
from Symphony No. 7

Ludwig van Beethoven
arranged by Douglas Court

Ludwig van Beethoven's (1770-1827) Seventh Symphony was written in 1812, and was first performed in Vienna in 1813 at a benefit concert for Australian and Bavarian soldiers wounded in Wellington's campaigns. The Allegretto section has a simple but relentless march rhythm, and was so popular it was encored at the first performance. In later years its popularity led to its use as a substitute for the slow movements of the Second and Eighth Symphonies.

GYPSY RONDO

Franz Joseph Haydn
arranged by James Curnow

Franz Joseph Haydn (1732-1809) was an Austrian composer whose life span encompassed both the Baroque and Classical periods. He was a central part of the establishment of the Classical Style. Because of his works, the symphony and string quartet came to life. He was a prolific composer of over 100 symphonies, numerous masses, operas, string quartets, chamber works, orchestral and choral works.

Little is known about the "Gypsy Rondo" except that it is one of Haydn's most frequently performed works for Young Pianists. A rondo is a musical form characterized by a repeated theme that alternates with other themes. "Gypsy Rondo" is an ABACA form.

TRUMPET TUNE

Henry Purcell
arranged by Stephen Bulla

Henry Purcell's (1659-1695) famous melody is heard most frequently as a processional or recessional at weddings, usually performed by solo trumpet and organ. The music is regal, dignified, and dramatic.

HUNGARIAN DANCE NO. 5

Johannes Brahms
arranged by Mike Hannickel

Johannes Brahms (1833-1897) was one of the greatest composers of the Romantic era. He was an ardent admirer of the music of Beethoven, and many consider him to be Beethoven's true successor in composition of both chamber music and symphonies.

Originally written for two pianos, Hungarian Dance No. 5 is among the most popular of Brahms' smaller works. The minor key, sudden tempo changes and energetic leaps of melody are characteristic of a time when 'exotic' music was a very popular entertainment.

PIZZICATO POLKA

Johann Jr. and Joseph Strauss
arranged by Mike Hannickel

The Strauss family repertoire of compositions is huge indeed. Johann Strauss (1804-49), the elder, and three sons, Johann Jr. (1825-99), Joseph (1827-70) and Eduard (1835-1916), were all prolific composers. Their combined output adds many hundreds of delightful pieces to the world of orchestral music.

To a musician, "pizzicato" means to pluck a string rather than bow it in order to produce a tone. Since wind instruments don't have strings they cannot truly perform "pizzicato". Winds do, however, have many ways to interpret each individual note. This transcription from the original string orchestra piece to a band version explores a few of these techniques.

AVE VERUM CORPUS

Wolfgang Amadeus Mozart
arranged by Timothy Johnson

AVE VERUM CORPUS is a motet that was written by Wolfgang Amadeus Mozart (1756-1792) during the last year of his life on June 17th, 1791. The piece was written for Anton Stoll, who was a teacher and choirmaster in Baden (near Vienna, Austria). Though it is one of Mozart's shortest works, it is considered one of his finest. Albert Einstein saw this motet as a coming together of Mozart's religious and personal life.

TRUMPET VOLUNTARY

(The Prince of Denmark's March)

Jeremiah Clarke
arranged by James Curnow

Little is known about Jeremiah Clarke's brief life (1674-1707), however it is known that he was an English composer and organist who served in several institutions including Winchester College and St. Paul's Cathedral in London. He composed church music, odes, songs, incidental music for the theater, and harpsichord pieces. Trumpet Voluntary, which is his best known work, is a majestic melody.

PEER GYNT SUITE NO. 1

Edvard Grieg
arranged by James Curnow

Edvard Grieg was born in Bergen, Norway in 1843 and, with the exception of tours as a guest conductor and soloist, lived there until his death in 1907. He was a celebrated international figure and considered to be Norway's greatest composer of the 19th century.

Henrik Ibsen wrote his extraordinary verse-drama, PEER GYNT, as a dramatic poem, without any thought of the theater. Only some years later did Ibsen think of arranging it for the stage. For this project, he sought the collaboration of Edvard Grieg who wrote several pieces of music for the stage production. Four of these pieces, taken from Grieg's Orchestral Suite #1, are represented in James Curnow's masterful arrangement of PEER GYNT SUITE:

1. ***Morning Mood*** – conjures up a picture of a fresh sunlit Scandinavian morning.
2. ***The Death of Ase*** – concludes the scene in Act III of the death of Peer's mother.
3. ***Anitra's Dance*** – an exotic mazurka danced by a Bedouin chief's daughter who Peer meets during his African adventure.
4. ***In the Hall of the Mountain King*** – portrays Peer's terrified escape in Act II from the royal hall of the trolls of the Norwegian uplands.

CLASSICS

FOR THE YOUNG CLARINET PLAYER

CONTENTS

Ludwig van Beethoven
ALLEGRETTO
from Symphony No. 7

Arr. **Douglas Court** (ASCAP)

GYPSY RONDO

Arr. **James Curnow** (ASCAP)

track 4

Copyright © 2001 by **Curnow Music Press, Inc.**

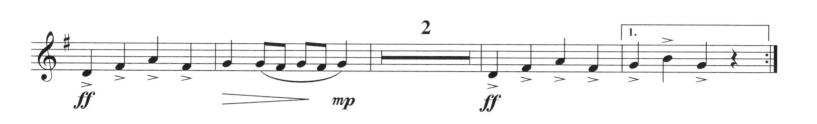

Henry Purcell
TRUMPET TUNE

Arr. **Stephen Bulla** (ASCAP)

Copyright © 2001 by **Curnow Music Press, Inc.**

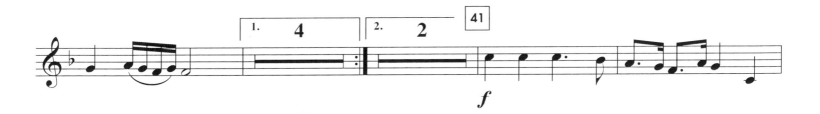

Johannes Brahms
HUNGARIAN DANCE NO. 5

track **6**

Arr. **Mike Hannickel** (ASCAP)

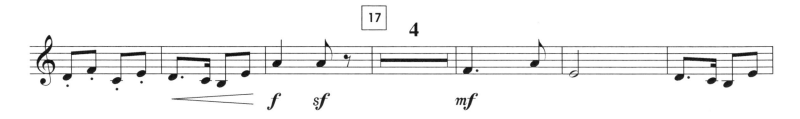

 Allegro

marc.

Slowly

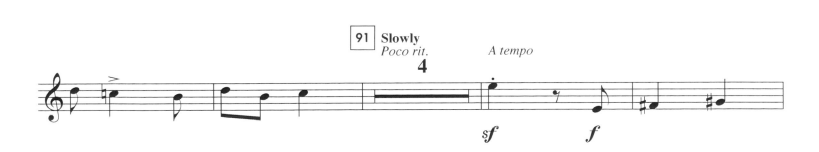

Johann Jr. and Joseph Strauss
PIZZICATO POLKA

Arr. **Mike Hannickel** (ASCAP)

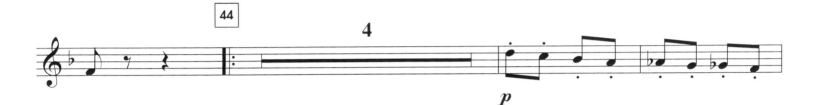

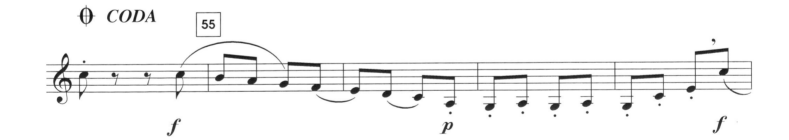

Wolfgang Amadeus Mozart
AVE VERUM CORPUS

Arr. **Timothy Johnson** (ASCAP)

Jeremiah Clarke
TRUMPET VOLUNTARY

Arr. **James Curnow** (ASCAP)

Copyright © 2001 by **Curnow Music Press, Inc.**

Edvard Grieg
PEER GYNT SUITE NO. 1

Arr. **James Curnow** (ASCAP)

1. Morning Mood

2. The Death of Ase

3. Anitra's Dance

4. In the Hall of the Mountain King